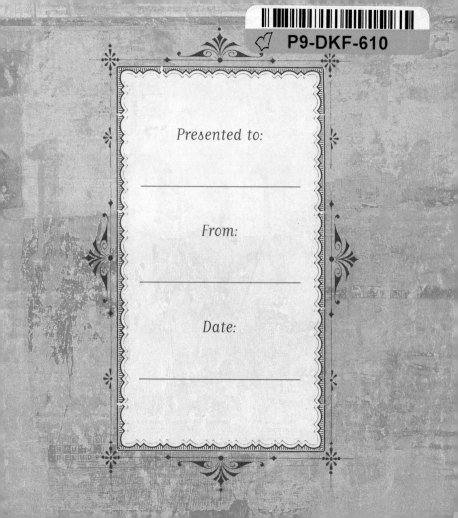

P9-DKF-610

Presented to:

_____

From:

_____

Date:

_____

TRAVELING LIGHT

FOR MOTHERS

Max Lucado

W PUBLISHING GROUP™

www.wpublishinggroup.com

A Division of Thomas Nelson, Inc.
www.ThomasNelson.com

Published by W Publishing Group, a unit of Thomas Nelson, Inc., P.O. Box 141000, Nashville, Tennessee 37214.

Unless otherwise indicated, Scripture quotations used in this book are from the Holy Bible, New Century Version, copyright © 1987, 1988, 1991 by W Publishing Group, Nashville, Tennessee 37214. Used by permission.

Other Scripture references are from the following sources:

The Living Bible (TLB), copyright © 1971 by Tyndale House Publishers, Wheaton, Illinois. Used by permission.

The Message (MSG), copyright © 1993. Used by permission of NavPress Publishing Group.

The New King James Version (NKJV), copyright © 1979, 1980, 1982, Thomas Nelson, Inc., Publishers.

The Jerusalem Bible (JB), copyright © 1968 by Darton, Longman, & Todd, Ltd., and Doubleday & Co., Inc.

The Holy Bible, New International Version (NIV), copyright © 1973, 1978, 1984, International Bible Society. Used by permission of Zondervan Bible Publishers.

The New English Bible (NEB), copyright © 1961, 1970 by the Delegates of the Oxford University Press and the Syndics of the Cambridge University Press, 1961, 1970. Reprinted by permission.

The Holy Bible, New Living Translation (NLT), copyright © 1996. Used by permission of Tyndale House Publishers, Inc., Wheaton, Illinois. All rights reserved.

ISBN 0-8499-9048-3

Printed in the United States of America

02 03 04 05 06 PHX 9 8 7 6 5 4 3 2

For my three nieces

Dana, Michelle, and Allison.

May God bless your mothering.

CONTENTS

1. MOM'S PURSE · 1

2. I'LL DO IT MY WAY

The Burden of Self-Reliance · 13

3. THE PRISON OF WANT

The Burden of Discontent · 25

4. I WILL GIVE YOU REST

The Burden of Weariness · 41

5. WHADDIFS AND HOWELLS

The Burden of Worry · 63

6. IT'S A JUNGLE OUT THERE

The Burden of Hopelessness · 83

7. A HEAVENLY EXCHANGE

The Burden of Guilt · 99

Notes · 117

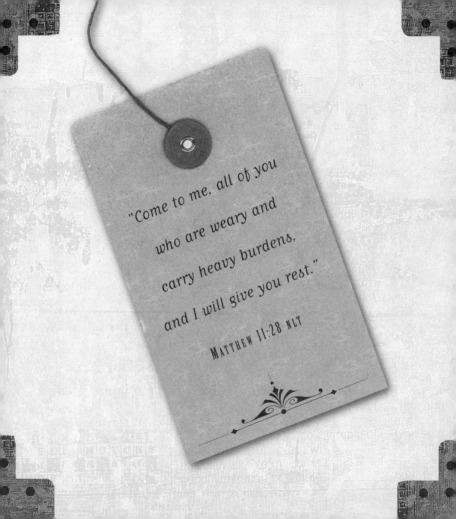

"Come to me, all of you who are weary and carry heavy burdens, and I will give you rest."

MATTHEW 11:28 NLT

MOM'S PURSE

I've never ceased to be amazed at what a mom can find in her purse. There's the typical stuff, like a tissue for a stuffy nose, a quarter for the gumball machine, a library card to check out a book. But then there's the incredible stuff, like a blowup beachball, a map of the entire United States, a collection of medicine that could cure any illness!

I guess moms learn early that they have to be prepared. It all starts with that diaper bag that has zippers galore and compartments begging to be filled so that no mother need be caught unprepared when spit-up (or a more unpleasant discharge) ruins the outfit and threatens to ruin the outing. From then on, moms seem to know how to pack backpacks for school, gym bags for games, footlockers for camp with anything and everything that might be needed.

Now, I've never carried a purse, but I've never been one to travel light.

I've tried. Believe me, I've tried. But ever since I stuck three fingers in the air and took the Boy Scout pledge to be prepared, I've been determined to be exactly that—prepared.

Prepared for a bar mitzvah, baby dedication, or costume party. Prepared to parachute behind enemy lines or enter a cricket tournament. And if, perchance, the Dalai Lama might be on my flight and invite me to dine in Tibet, I carry snowshoes. One has to be prepared.

I don't know how to travel without granola bars, sodas, and rain gear. I don't know how to travel without flashlights and a generator and a global tracking system. I don't know how to travel without an ice chest of wieners. What if I stumble upon a backyard barbecue? To bring nothing to the party would be rude.

I don't know how to travel light. But I need to learn.

I need to learn to travel light.

You're wondering why I can't. *Loosen up!* you're thinking. *You can't enjoy a journey carrying so much stuff. Why don't you just drop all that luggage?*

Funny you should ask. I'd like to inquire the same of

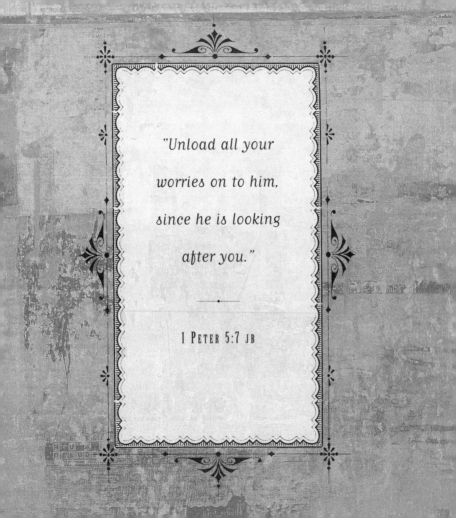

"Unload all your worries on to him, since he is looking after you."

1 PETER 5:7 JB

you. Haven't you been known to pack your bag with some unnecessary items?

Odds are, you did this morning. Somewhere between the first step on the floor and the last step out the door, you stuffed your bag full. It wasn't a bag made of leather, but the one in the mind. And you didn't fill it with books or Band-Aids or Binaca, you filled it with burdens. The kind of burdens that moms carry.

The suitcase of guilt. A sack of discontent. You drape a duffel bag of weariness on one shoulder and a hanging bag of worry on the other. No wonder you're so tired at the end of the day. Toting those kinds of bags is exhausting.

What you were saying to me, God is saying to you, "Set that stuff down! You're carrying burdens you don't need to bear."

"Come to me," he invites, "all of you who are weary

and carry heavy burdens, and I will give you rest" (Matt. 11:28 NLT).

If we let him, God will lighten our loads . . . but how do we let him? May I invite an old friend to show us? The first few verses of the Twenty-third Psalm.

> The LORD is my shepherd;
>   I shall not want.
> He makes me to lie down in green pastures;
> He leads me beside the still waters.
> He restores my soul;
> He leads me in the paths of righteousness
> For His name's sake. (NKJV)

Have you been packing your purse with some burdens

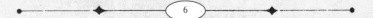

of your own? Do you think God might use David's psalm to lighten your load? *Traveling light means trusting God with the burdens you were never intended to bear.*

Why don't you try traveling light? Try it for the sake of those you love. Have you ever considered the impact that excess baggage has on relationships? We've made this point at our church by virtue of a drama. A wedding is reenacted in which we hear the thoughts of the bride and groom. The groom enters, laden with luggage. A bag dangles from every appendage. And each bag is labeled: guilt, anger, arrogance, insecurities. This fellow is loaded. As he stands on the altar, the audience hears him thinking, *Finally, a woman who will help me carry all my burdens. She's so strong, so stable, so . . .*

As his thoughts continue, hers begin. She enters, wearing a wedding gown but, like her fiancé, covered with luggage.

Pulling a hanging bag, shouldering a carry-on, hauling a makeup kit, a paper sack—everything you could imagine and everything labeled. She has her own bags: prejudice, loneliness, disappointments. And her expectations? Listen to what she is thinking: *Just a few more minutes and I've got me a man. No more counselors. No more group sessions. So long, discouragement and worry. I won't be seeing you anymore. He's going to fix me.*

Finally they stand at the altar, lost in a mountain of luggage. They smile their way through the ceremony, but when given the invitation to kiss each other, they can't. How do you embrace someone if your arms are full of bags?

For the sake of those you love, learn to set them down.

And, for the sake of the God you serve, do the same. He wants to use you, you know. But how can he if you are

"Traveling light means trusting God with the burdens you were never intended to bear."

exhausted? This truth came home to me yesterday after-noon on a run. Preparing for a jog, I couldn't decide what to wear. The sun was out, but the wind was chilly. The sky was clear, but the forecast said rain. Jacket or sweatshirt? The Boy Scout within me prevailed. I wore both.

I grabbed my Walkman but couldn't decide which tape to bring. A sermon or music? You guessed it, I took both. Needing to stay in touch with my kids, I carried a cell phone. So no one would steal my car, I pocketed my keys. As a precaution against thirst, I brought along some drink money in a pouch. I looked more like a pack mule than a runner! Within half a mile I was peeling off the jacket and hiding it in a bush. That kind of weight will slow you down.

What's true in jogging is true in faith. God has a great race for you to run. Under his care you will go where you've never been and serve in ways you've never dreamed. But you have to drop some stuff. How can you share grace if you are full of guilt? How can you offer comfort if you are disheartened? How can you lift someone else's load if your arms are full with your own?

For the sake of those you love, travel light.

For the sake of the God you serve, travel light.

For the sake of your own joy, travel light.

There are certain weights in life you simply cannot carry. Your Lord is asking you to set them down and trust him. He is the father at the baggage claim. When a dad sees his five-year-old son trying to drag the family trunk off the carousel, what does he say? The father will say to his son what God is saying to you.

"Set it down, child. I'll carry that one."

What do you say we take God up on his offer? We just might find ourselves traveling a little lighter.

By the way, I may have overstated my packing problems. (I don't usually take snowshoes.) But I can't overstate God's promise: "Unload all your worries on to him, since he is looking after you" (1 Pet. 5:7 JB).

t w o

I'LL DO IT MY WAY

———•———

The Burden of Self-Reliance

The LORD is my shepherd.

—PSALM 23:1 NKJV

If there's one thing I've noticed about moms, it's that they seem to know how to take care of things. Whatever the problem, they seem to be able to sew it up,

13

wash it down, work it over. Moms are resourceful. And sometimes, that resourcefulness can fool them into becoming self-reliant. They begin to think:

I don't need advice.

I can handle this myself.

I don't need a shepherd, thank you.

Can you relate?

We humans want to do things our way. Forget the easy way. Forget the common way. Forget the best way. Forget God's way. We want to do things *our* way.

And, according to the Bible, that's precisely our problem. "We all have wandered away like sheep; each of us has gone his own way" (Isa. 53:6).

You wouldn't think sheep would be obstinate. Of all God's animals, the sheep is the least able to take care of himself.

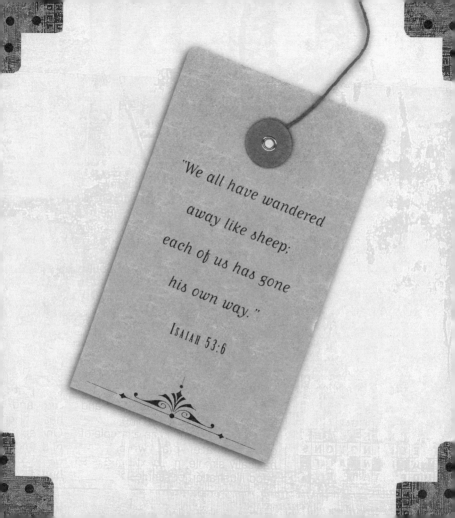

"We all have wandered away like sheep; each of us has gone his own way."

ISAIAH 53:6

Sheep are dumb! Have you ever met a sheep trainer? Ever seen sheep tricks? Know anyone who has taught his sheep to roll over? Ever witnessed a circus sideshow featuring "Mazadon and his jumping sheep"? No. Sheep are just too dumb.

And defenseless. They have no fangs or claws. They can't bite you or outrun you. That's why you never see sheep as team mascots. We've heard of the St. Louis Rams and the Chicago Bulls and the Seattle Seahawks, but the New York Lambs? Who wants to be a lamb? You couldn't even stir up a decent yell for the cheerleaders.

> We are the sheep.
> We don't make a peep.
> Victory is yours to keep.
> But count us if you want to sleep.

What's more, sheep are dirty. A cat can clean itself. So can a dog. We see a bird in a birdbath or a bear in a river. But sheep? They get dirty and stay that way.

Couldn't David have thought of a better metaphor? Surely he could have. After all, he outran Saul and out-gunned Goliath. Why didn't he choose something other than sheep?

How about:

"The Lord is my commander in chief, and I am his warrior." There. We like that better. A warrior gets a uniform and a weapon, maybe even a medal.

Or, "The Lord is my inspiration, and I am his singer." We are in God's choir; what a flattering assignment.

Or, "The Lord is my king, and I am his ambassador." Who wouldn't like to be a spokesperson for God?

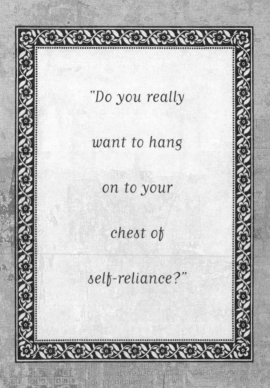

"Do you really

want to hang

on to your

chest of

self-reliance?"

Everyone stops when the ambassador speaks. Everyone listens when God's minstrel sings. Everyone applauds when God's warrior passes.

But who notices when God's sheep show up? Who notices when the sheep sing or speak or act? Only one person notices. The shepherd. And that is precisely David's point.

When David, who was a warrior, minstrel, and ambassador for God, searched for an illustration of God, he remembered his days as a shepherd. He remembered how he lavished attention on the sheep day and night. How he slept with them and watched over them.

And the way he cared for the sheep reminded him of the way God cares for us. David rejoiced to say, "The LORD is my shepherd," and in so doing he proudly implied, "I am his sheep."

Still uncomfortable with being considered a sheep? Will you humor me and take a simple quiz? See if you succeed in self-reliance. Raise your hand if any of the following describe you.

You can control your moods. You're never grumpy or sullen. You can't relate to Jekyll and Hyde. You're always upbeat and upright. Does that describe you? No? Well, let's try another.

You are at peace with everyone. Every relationship as sweet as fudge. Even your old flames speak highly of you. Love all and loved by all. Is that you? If not, how about this description?

You have no fears. Call you the Teflon toughie. Wall Street plummets—no problem. Heart condition discovered—yawn. World War III starts—what's for dinner? Does this describe you?

You need no forgiveness. Never made a mistake. As square as

"David rejoiced
to say, 'The Lord is
my shepherd,'
and in so soing
he proudly implied,
'I am his sheep.'"

a game of checkers. As clean as Grandma's kitchen. Never cheated, never lied, never lied about cheating. Is that you? No?

Let's evaluate this. You can't control your moods. A few of your relationships are shaky. You have fears and faults. Hmmm. Do you really want to hang on to your chest of self-reliance? Sounds to me as if you could use a shepherd. Otherwise, you might end up with a Twenty-third Psalm like this:

> I am my own shepherd. I am always in need.
> I stumble from mall to mall and shrink to shrink,
> seeking relief but never finding it.
> I creep through the valley of the shadow of death and
> fall apart.
> I fear everything from pesticides to power lines, and I'm
> starting to act like my mother.

I go down to the weekly staff meeting and am
surrounded by enemies. I go home, and even my
goldfish scowls at me.
I anoint my headache with Extra-Strength Tylenol.
My Jack Daniels runneth over.
Surely misery and misfortune will follow me, and I will
live in self-doubt for the rest of my lonely life.

Why is it that the ones who most need a shepherd resist
him so?

Ah, now there is a question for the super self-sufficient
mom. Scripture says, "Do it God's way." Experience says,
"Do it God's way."

And, every so often, we do.

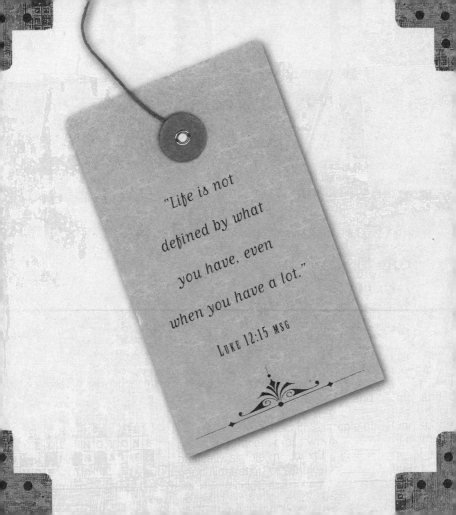

"Life is not defined by what you have, even when you have a lot."

Luke 12:15 MSG

three

THE PRISON OF WANT

The Burden of Discontent

The LORD is my shepherd; I shall not want.

—PSALM 23:1 NKJV

Come with me to the most populated prison in the world. The facility has more inmates than bunks. More prisoners than plates. More residents than resources.

Come with me to the world's most oppressive prison. Just ask the inmates; they will tell you. They are overworked and underfed. Their walls are bare and bunks are hard.

No prison is so populated, no prison so oppressive, and, what's more, no prison is so permanent. Most inmates never leave. They never escape. They never get released. They serve a life sentence in this overcrowded, underprovisioned facility.

The name of the prison? You'll see it over the entrance. Rainbowed over the gate are four cast-iron letters that spell out its name:

W-A-N-T

The prison of want. You've seen her prisoners. They are "in want." They want something. They want something bigger. Nicer. Faster. Thinner. They want.

They don't want much, mind you. They want just one thing. One new couch. One new car. One new house. One new spouse. They don't want much. They want just one.

And when they have "one," they will be happy. And they are right—they will be happy. When they have "one," they will leave the prison. But then it happens. The couch gets a spot. The new job gets old. The neighbors buy a larger television set. The new spouse has bad habits. The sizzle fizzles, and before you know it, another ex-con breaks parole and returns to jail.

Are you in prison? You are if you feel better when you have more and worse when you have less. You are if joy is one delivery away, one transfer away, one award away, or one makeover away. If your happiness comes from something

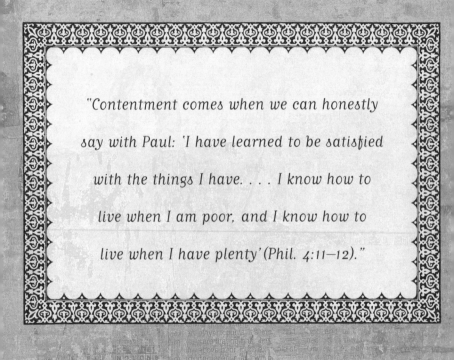

"Contentment comes when we can honestly say with Paul: 'I have learned to be satisfied with the things I have. . . . I know how to live when I am poor, and I know how to live when I have plenty' (Phil. 4:11–12)."

you deposit, drive, drink, or digest, then face it—you are in prison, the prison of want.

That's the bad news. The good news is, you have a visitor. And your visitor has a message that can get you paroled. Make your way to the receiving room. Take your seat in the chair, and look across the table at the psalmist David. He motions for you to lean forward. "I have a secret to tell you," he whispers, "the secret of satisfaction. 'The LORD is my shepherd; I shall not want'" (Ps. 23:1 NKJV).

David has found the pasture where discontent goes to die. It's as if he is saying, "What I have in God is greater than what I don't have in life."

You think you and I could learn to say the same?

Think for just a moment about the things you own. Think about the house you have, the car you drive, the money you've saved. Think about the jewelry you've inherited and the stocks you've traded and the clothes you've purchased. Envision all your stuff, and let me remind you of two biblical truths.

Your stuff isn't yours. Ask any coroner. Ask any embalmer. Ask any funeral-home director. No one takes anything with him. When one of the wealthiest men in history, John D. Rockefeller, died, his accountant was asked, "How much did John D. leave?" The accountant's reply? "All of it."[1]

"Naked a man comes from his mother's womb, and as he comes, so he departs. He takes nothing from his labor that he can carry in his hand" (Eccles. 5:15 NIV).

All that stuff—it's not yours. And you know what else about all that stuff? *It's not you.* Who you are has nothing to do with the clothes you wear or the car you drive. Jesus said,

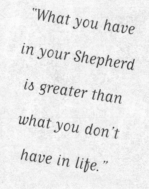

"What you have
in your Shepherd
is greater than
what you don't
have in life."

TICKET: | DATE:

TRAVELING LIGHT

"Life is not defined by what you have, even when you have a lot" (Luke 12:15 MSG). Heaven does not know you as the woman with the big house. Heaven knows your heart. "The LORD does not look at the things man looks at. Man looks at the outward appearance, but the LORD looks at the heart" (1 Sam. 16:7 NIV). When God thinks of you, he may see your compassion, your devotion, your tenderness or quick mind, but he doesn't think of your things.

And when you think of you, you shouldn't either. Define yourself by your stuff, and you'll feel good when you have a lot and bad when you don't. Contentment comes when we can honestly say with Paul: "I have learned to be satisfied with the things I have. . . . I know how to live when I am poor, and I know how to live when I have plenty" (Phil. 4:11–12).

Doug McKnight could say those words. At the age of

thirty-two he was diagnosed with multiple sclerosis. Over the next sixteen years it would cost him his career, his mobility, and eventually his life. Because of MS, he couldn't feed himself or walk; he battled depression and fear. But through it all, Doug never lost his sense of gratitude. Evidence of this was seen in his prayer list. Friends in his congregation asked him to compile a list of requests so they could intercede for him. His response included eighteen blessings for which to be grateful and six concerns for which to be prayerful. His blessings outweighed his needs by three times. Doug McKnight had learned to be content.[2]

So had the leper on the island of Tobago. A short-term missionary met her on a mission trip. On the final day, he was leading worship in a leper colony. He asked if anyone had a favorite song. When he did, a woman turned around,

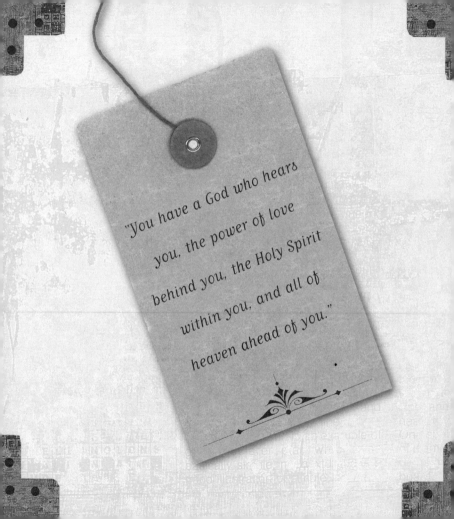

"You have a God who hears you, the power of love behind you, the Holy Spirit within you, and all of heaven ahead of you."

and he saw the most disfigured face he'd ever seen. She had no ears and no nose. Her lips were gone. But she raised a fingerless hand and asked, "Could we sing 'Count Your Many Blessings'?"

The missionary started the song but couldn't finish. Someone later commented, "I suppose you'll never be able to sing the song again." He answered, "No, I'll sing it again. Just never in the same way."[3]

Are you hoping that a change in circumstances will bring a change in your attitude? If so, you are in prison, and you need to learn a secret of traveling light. *What you have in your Shepherd is greater than what you don't have in life.*

May I meddle for a moment? What is the one thing separating you from joy? How do you fill in this blank: "I will be happy when _____"? When I am healed.

When I am thinner. When I have another child. When my children leave home. When I am rich. How would you finish that statement?

Now, with your answer firmly in mind, answer this. If your ship never comes in, if your dream never comes true, if the situation never changes, could you be happy? If not, then you are sleeping in the cold cell of discontent. You are in prison. And you need to know what you have in your Shepherd.

You have a God who hears you, the power of love behind you, the Holy Spirit within you, and all of heaven ahead of you. If you have the Shepherd, you have grace for every sin, direction for every turn, a candle for every corner, and an anchor for every storm. You have everything you need.

And who can take it from you? Can leukemia infect

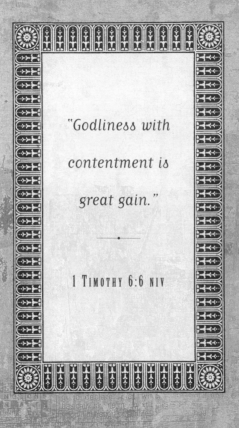

"Godliness with contentment is great gain."

1 TIMOTHY 6:6 NIV

your salvation? Can bankruptcy impoverish your prayers? A tornado might take your earthly house, but will it touch your heavenly home?

And look at your position. Why clamor for prestige and power? Are you not already privileged to be part of the greatest work in history—raising the next generation to love and serve God?

A man once went to a minister for counseling. He was in the midst of a financial collapse. "I've lost everything," he bemoaned.

"Oh, I'm so sorry to hear that you've lost your faith."

"No," the man corrected him, "I haven't lost my faith."

"Well, then I'm sad to hear that you've lost your character."

"I didn't say that," he corrected. "I still have my character."

"I'm so sorry to hear that you've lost your salvation."

"That's not what I said," the man objected. "I haven't lost my salvation."

"You have your faith, your character, your salvation. Seems to me," the minister observed, "that you've lost none of the things that really matter."

We haven't either. You and I could pray like the Puritan. He sat down to a meal of bread and water. He bowed his head and declared, "All this and Jesus too?"

Can't we be equally content? Paul says that "godliness with contentment is great gain" (1 Tim. 6:6 NIV). When we surrender to God the cumbersome sack of discontent, we don't just give up something; we gain something. God replaces it with a lightweight, tailor-made, sorrow-resistant attaché of gratitude.

What will you gain with contentment? You may gain your marriage. You may gain precious hours with your children. You may gain your self-respect. You may gain joy. You may gain the faith to say, "The LORD is my shepherd; I shall not want."

Try saying it slowly. "The LORD is my shepherd; I shall not want."

Again, "The LORD is my shepherd; I shall not want."

Again, "The LORD is my shepherd; I shall not want."

Shhhhhhh. Did you hear something? I think I did. I'm not sure . . . but I think I heard the opening of a jail door.

I WILL GIVE YOU REST

The Burden of Weariness

He makes me to lie down in green pastures.

—PSALM 23:2 NKJV

Moms, did the title of this chapter perk you up faster than your morning latté? I hope so, because I'll bet you could use a little rest just about now. By the time you've got the house humming and the kids running, by the

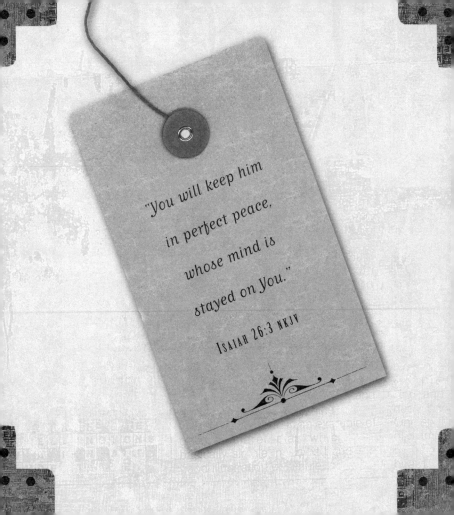

"You will keep him
in perfect peace,
whose mind is
stayed on You."

ISAIAH 26:3 NKJV

time the bills are paid, meals are made, and life begins to look orderly, it all starts over again. You need a break, don't you? You're not alone. Read the consequences of the burden; then guess the cause:

- It afflicts 70 million Americans and is faulted for 38,000 deaths each year.

- The condition annually costs the U.S. $70 billion worth of productivity.

- Teenagers suffer from it. Studies show that 64 percent of teens blame it for poor school performance.

- Middle agers face it. Researchers say the most severe cases occur between ages thirty and forty.

- Senior citizens are afflicted by it. One study suggests

that the condition impacts 50 percent of the over-sixty-five population.

- Treatments involve everything from mouth guards to herbal teas to medication.[1]

Any idea what's being described?

Chemical abuse? Divorce? Long sermons? None of those answers are correct, though the last one was a good hunch. The answer may surprise you. Insomnia. America can't get to sleep.

For most of my life I secretly snickered at the thought of sleep difficulties. My problem was not in going to sleep. My problem was staying awake. But a few years ago I went to bed one night, closed my eyes, and nothing happened. I

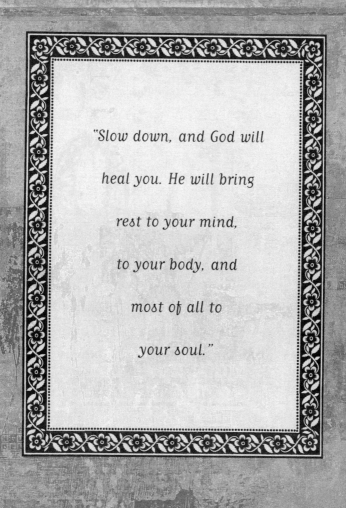

"Slow down, and God will

heal you. He will bring

rest to your mind,

to your body, and

most of all to

your soul."

didn't fall asleep. Rather than slow to a halt, my mind kicked into high gear. A thousand and one obligations rushed at me. Midnight passed, and I was still awake. I drank some milk, returned to bed. I was still awake. I woke up Denalyn, using the blue ribbon of dumb questions, "Are you awake?" She told me to quit thinking about things. So I did. I quit thinking about things and started thinking about people. But as I thought of people, I thought of what those people were doing. They were sleeping. That made me mad and kept me awake. Finally, somewhere in the early hours of the morning, having been initiated into the fraternity of seventy million sleepless Americans, I dozed off.

I don't snicker at the thought of sleep difficulties anymore. Nor do I question the inclusion of the verse about rest in the Twenty-third Psalm.

People with too much work and too little sleep step over to the baggage claim of life and grab the duffel bag of weariness. You don't carry this one. You don't hoist it onto your shoulder and stride down the street. You drag it as you would a stubborn St. Bernard. Weariness wearies.

Why are we so tired? Have you read a newspaper lately? We long to have the life of Huck and Tom on the Mississippi, but look at us riding the white waters of the Rio Grande. Forks in the river. Rocks in the water. Heart attacks, betrayal, credit-card debt, and custody battles. Huck and Tom didn't have to face these kinds of things. We do, however, and they keep us awake. And since we can't sleep, we have a second problem.

Our bodies are tired. Think about it. If seventy million Americans aren't sleeping enough, what does that mean? That means one-third of our country is dozing off at work,

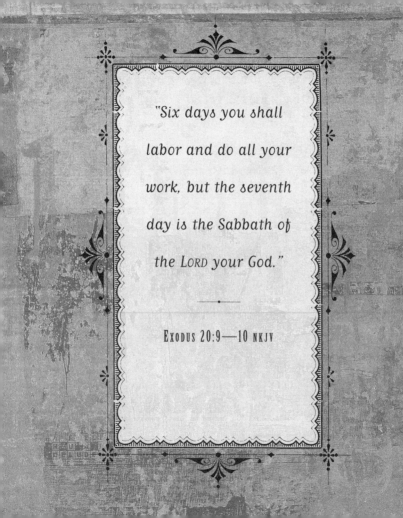

"Six days you shall labor and do all your work, but the seventh day is the Sabbath of the LORD your God."

Exodus 20:9—10 NKJV

napping through class, or sleeping at the wheel (fifteen hundred road deaths per year are blamed on heavy-eyed truck drivers). Some even snooze while reading Lucado books. (Hard to fathom, I know.) Thirty tons of aspirins, sleeping pills, and tranquilizers are consumed every day![2] The energy gauges on the dashboards of our foreheads say empty.

Were we to invite an alien to solve our problem, he'd suggest a simple solution—everybody go to sleep. We'd laugh at him. He doesn't understand the way we work. Literally. He doesn't understand *the way* we work. We work hard. There is money to be made. Degrees to be earned. Ladders to be climbed. In our book, busyness is next to godliness. We idolize Thomas Edison, who claimed he could live on fifteen-minute naps. Somehow we forget to mention Albert Einstein, who averaged eleven hours of sleep a night.[3] In 1910 Americans slept nine hours a night; today we sleep seven and are proud of it. And we are tired because of it. Our minds are tired. Our bodies are tired. But much more important, our souls are tired.

We are eternal creatures, and we ask eternal questions: Where did I come from? Where am I going? What is the meaning of life? What is right? What is wrong? Is there life after death? These are the primal questions of the soul. And left unanswered, such questions will steal our rest.

Only one other living creature has as much trouble resting as we do. Not dogs. They doze. Not bears. They hibernate. Cats invented the catnap, and the sloth slumbers twenty hours a day. (So *that's* what I was rooming with my sophomore year in college.) Most animals know how to rest. There is one exception. These creatures are woolly,

"Can you imagine the satisfaction in the heart of the shepherd when, with work completed, he sees his sheep rest in the tender grass?"

simpleminded, and slow. No, not husbands on Saturday—sheep! Sheep can't sleep.

For sheep to sleep, everything must be just right. No predators. No tension in the flock. No bugs in the air. No hunger in the belly.[4] Everything has to be just so.

Unfortunately, sheep cannot find safe pasture, nor can they spray insecticide, deal with the frictions, or find food. They need help. They need a shepherd to lead them and help them "lie down in green pastures." Without a shepherd, they can't rest.

Without a shepherd, neither can we.

In the second verse of the Twenty-third Psalm, David the poet becomes David the artist. His quill becomes a brush, his parchment a canvas, and his words paint a picture. A flock of sheep on folded legs, encircling a shepherd.

Bellies nestled deep in the long shoots of grass. A still pond on one side, the watching shepherd on the other. "He makes me to lie down in green pastures; He leads me beside the still waters" (Ps. 23:2 NKJV).

Note the two pronouns preceding the two verbs. *He* makes me . . . *He* leads me . . .

Who is the active one? Who is in charge? The shepherd. The shepherd selects the trail and prepares the pasture. The sheep's job—our job—is to watch the shepherd. With our eyes on our Shepherd, we'll be able to get some sleep. "You will keep him in perfect peace, whose mind is stayed on You" (Isa. 26:3 NKJV).

May I show you something? Flip to the back of this book, and look at an empty page. When you look at it, what do you see? What you see is a white piece of paper.

Now place a dot in the center of the sheet. Look at it again. Now what do you see? You see the dot, don't you? And isn't that our problem? We let the dark marks eclipse the white space.

We see the waves of the water rather than the Savior walking through them. We focus on our paltry provisions rather than on the One who can feed five thousand hungry people. We concentrate on the dark Fridays of crucifixion and miss the bright Sundays of resurrection.

Change your focus and relax.

And while you are at it, change your schedule and rest!

The other day my wife met a friend at a restaurant for coffee. The two entered the parking lot at the same time. When Denalyn stepped out of her car, she saw her friend waving her over. Denalyn thought she was saying something, but she couldn't hear a word. A jackhammer was pounding pavement only a few feet away. She walked toward her friend, who, as it turned out, was just saying hello, and the two entered the restaurant.

When it came time to leave, my wife couldn't find her keys. She looked in her purse, on the floor, in her friend's car. Finally, when she went to her car, there they were. Not only were the keys in the ignition, the car was running. It had been running the entire time she and her friend were in the café.

Denalyn blames the oversight on the noise. "Everything was so loud, I forgot to turn it off."

The world gets that way. Life can get so loud we forget to shut it down. Maybe that's why God made such a big deal about rest in the Ten Commandments.

Since you did so well on the dot exercise, let me give you another. Of the ten declarations carved in the tablets, which one occupies the most space? Murder? Adultery? Stealing? You'd think so. Certainly each is worthy of ample coverage. But curiously, these commands are tributes to brevity. God needed only five English words to condemn adultery and four to denounce thievery and murder.

But when he came to the topic of rest, one sentence would not suffice.

Remember the Sabbath day, to keep it holy. Six days you shall labor and do all your work, but the seventh day is the Sabbath of the LORD your God. In it, you shall do no work: you, nor your son, nor your daughter, nor your male servant, nor your female servant, nor your cattle, nor your stranger who is within your gates. For in six days the LORD made the heavens and the earth, the sea, and all that is in them, and rested the seventh day. Therefore the LORD blessed the Sabbath day and hallowed it. (Exod. 20:8–11 NKJV)

God knows us so well. He can see the store owner reading this verse and musing, "Somebody needs to work that day. If I can't, my son will." So God says, *Nor your son.* "Then my daughter will." *Nor your daughter.* "Then maybe an employee." *Nor them.* "I guess I'll have to send my cow to run the store, or maybe I'll find some stranger to help me." *No,* God says. *One day of the week you will say no to work and yes to worship. You will slow and sit down and lie down and rest.*

Still we object. "But . . . but . . . but . . . who is going to run the store?" "What about my grades?" "I've got my sales quota." We offer up one reason after another, but God silences them all with a poignant reminder: "In six days the LORD made the heavens and the earth, the sea, and all that is in them, and rested the seventh day." God's message is plain: "If creation didn't crash when I rested, it won't crash when you do."

Repeat these words after me: It is not my job to run the world.

A century ago Charles Spurgeon gave this advice to his preaching students:

Even beasts of burden must be turned out to grass occasionally; the very sea pauses at ebb and flood; earth keeps the Sabbath of the wintry months; and man, even when

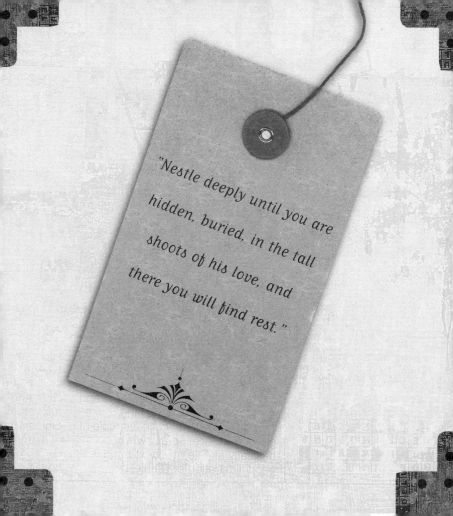

"Nestle deeply until you are hidden, buried, in the tall shoots of his love, and there you will find rest."

exalted to God's ambassador, must rest or faint, must trim his lamp or let it burn low; must recruit his vigor or grow prematurely old. . . . In the long run we shall do more by sometimes doing less.[5]

The bow cannot always be bent without fear of breaking. For a field to bear fruit, it must occasionally lie fallow. And for you to be healthy, you must rest. Slow down, and God will heal you. He will bring rest to your mind, to your body, and most of all to your soul. He will lead you to green pastures.

Green pastures were not the natural terrain of Judea. The hills around Bethlehem where David kept his flock were not lush and green. Even today they are white and parched. Any green pasture in Judea is the work of some shepherd. He has cleared the rough, rocky land. Stumps have been torn out, and brush has been burned. Irrigation. Cultivation. Such are the work of a shepherd.

Hence, when David says, "He makes me to lie down in green pastures," he is saying, "My Shepherd makes me lie down in his finished work." With his own pierced hands, Jesus created a pasture for the soul. He tore out the thorny underbrush of condemnation. He pried loose the huge boulders of sin. In their place he planted seeds of grace and dug ponds of mercy.

And he invites us to rest there. Can you imagine the satisfaction in the heart of the shepherd when, with work completed, he sees his sheep rest in the tender grass?

Can you imagine the satisfaction in the heart of God when we do the same? His pasture is his gift to us. This is not a pasture that you have made. Nor is it a pasture that you deserve. It is a gift of God. "For it is by grace you have been saved, through faith—and this not from yourselves, it is the gift of God" (Eph. 2:8 NIV).

In a world rocky with human failure, there is a land lush with divine mercy. Your Shepherd invites you there. He wants you to lie down. Nestle deeply until you are hidden, buried, in the tall shoots of his love, and there you will find rest.

WHADDIFS AND HOWELLS

The Burden of Worry

He leads me beside the still waters.

—PSALM 23:2 NKJV

Your ten-year-old is worried. So anxious he can't eat. So worried he can't sleep. "What's wrong?" you inquire. He shakes his head and moans, "I don't even have a pension plan."

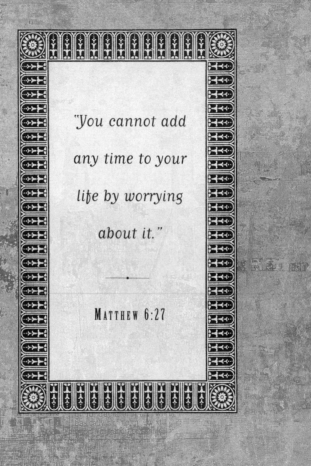

"You cannot add any time to your life by worrying about it."

MATTHEW 6:27

Or your four-year-old is crying in bed. "What's wrong, sweetheart?" She whimpers, "I'll never pass college chemistry."

Your eight-year-old's face is stress-struck. "I'll be a rotten parent. What if I set a poor example for my kids?"

How would you respond to such statements? Besides calling a child psychologist, your response would be emphatic: "You're too young to worry about those things. When the time comes, you'll know what to do."

Fortunately, most kids don't have such thoughts.

Unfortunately, we adults have more than our share. Worry is the burlap bag of burdens. It's overflowing with "whaddifs" and "howells." "Whaddif it rains at my wedding?" "Howell I know when to discipline my kids?" "Whaddif I marry a guy who snores?" "Howell we pay our baby's tuition?" "Whaddif, after all my dieting, they learn that lettuce is fattening and chocolate isn't?"

The burlap bag of worry. Cumbersome. Chunky. Unattractive. Scratchy. Hard to get a handle on. Irritating to carry and impossible to give away. No one wants your worries.

The truth be told, you don't want them either. No one has to remind you of the high cost of anxiety. (But I will anyway.) Worry divides the mind. The biblical word for *worry (merimnao)* is a compound of two Greek words, *merizo* ("to divide") and *nous* ("the mind"). Anxiety splits our energy between today's priorities and tomorrow's problems. Part of our mind is on the now; the rest is on the not yet. The result is half-minded living.

That's not the only result. Worrying is not a disease, but

"God is leading you. Leave tomorrow's problems until tomorrow."

TICKET:

DATE:

TRAVELING LIGHT

it causes diseases. It has been connected to high blood pressure, heart trouble, blindness, migraine headaches, thyroid malfunctions, and a host of stomach disorders.

Anxiety is an expensive habit. Of course, it might be worth the cost if it worked. But it doesn't. Our frets are futile. Jesus said, "You cannot add any time to your life by worrying about it" (Matt. 6:27). Worry has never brightened a day, solved a problem, or cured a disease.

How can a person deal with anxiety? You might try what one fellow did. He worried so much that he decided to hire someone to do his worrying for him. He found a man who agreed to be his hired worrier for a salary of $200,000 per year. After the man accepted the job, his first question to his boss was, "Where are you going to get $200,000 per year?" To which the man responded, "That's your worry."

Sadly, worrying is one job you can't farm out, but you can overcome it. There is no better place to begin than in verse 2 of the Shepherd Psalm.

"He leads me beside the still waters," David declares. And, in case we missed the point, he repeats the phrase in the next verse: "He leads me in the paths of righteousness."

"He leads me." God isn't behind me, yelling, "Go!" He is ahead of me, bidding, "Come!" He is in front, clearing the path, cutting the brush, showing the way. Just before the curve, he says, "Turn here." Prior to the rise, he motions, "Step up here." Standing next to the rocks, he warns, "Watch your step here."

He leads us. He tells us what we need to know when we need to know it. As a New Testament writer would affirm: "We will find grace to help us *when we need it*" (Heb. 4:16 NLT, emphasis mine).

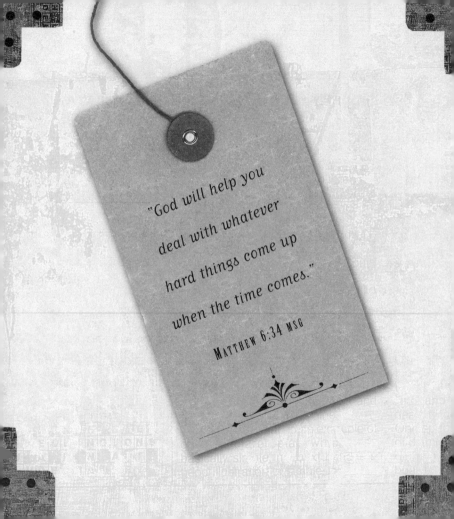

"God will help you deal with whatever hard things come up when the time comes."

MATTHEW 6:34 MSG

Listen to a different translation: "Let us therefore boldly approach the throne of our gracious God, where we may receive mercy and in his grace find *timely help*" (Heb. 4:16 NEB, emphasis mine).

God's help is timely. He helps us the same way a father gives plane tickets to his family. When I travel with my kids, I carry all our tickets in my satchel. When the moment comes to board the plane, I stand between the attendant and the child. As each daughter passes, I place a ticket in her hand. She, in turn, gives the ticket to the attendant. Each one receives the ticket in the nick of time.

What I do for my daughters God does for you. He places himself between you and the need. And at the right time, he gives you the ticket. Wasn't this the promise he gave his disciples? "When you are arrested and judged, don't worry ahead of time about what you should say. Say whatever *is given you to say at that time,* because it will not really be you speaking; it will be the Holy Spirit" (Mark 13:11, emphasis mine).

Isn't this the message God gave the children of Israel? He promised to supply them with manna each day. But he told them to collect only one day's supply at a time. Those who disobeyed and collected enough for two days found themselves with rotten manna. The only exception to the rule was the day prior to the Sabbath. On Friday they could gather twice as much. Otherwise, God would give them what they needed, in their time of need.

God leads us. God will do the right thing at the right time. And what a difference that makes.

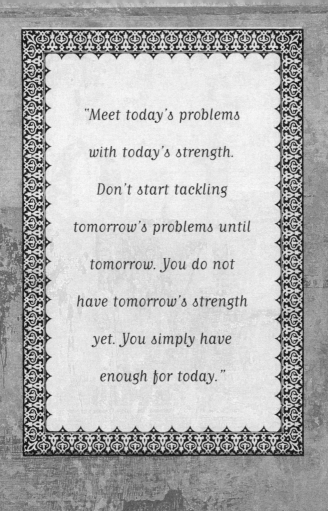

"Meet today's problems
with today's strength.
Don't start tackling
tomorrow's problems until
tomorrow. You do not
have tomorrow's strength
yet. You simply have
enough for today."

Since I know his provision is timely, I can enjoy the present.

"Give your entire attention to what God is doing right now, and don't get worked up about what may or may not happen tomorrow. God will help you deal with whatever hard things come up when the time comes" (Matt. 6:34 MSG).

That last phrase is worthy of your highlighter: "when the time comes."

"I don't know what I'll do if my husband dies." You will, *when the time comes.*

"When my children leave the house, I don't think I can take it." It won't be easy, but strength will arrive *when the time comes.*

The key is this: Meet today's problems with today's strength. Don't start tackling tomorrow's problems until tomorrow. You do not have tomorrow's strength yet. You simply have enough for today.

More than eighty years ago a great Canadian man of medicine, Sir William Osler, delivered a speech to the students of Yale University entitled "A Way of Life." In the message he related an event that occurred while he was aboard an ocean liner.

One day while he was visiting with the ship's captain, a loud, piercing alarm sounded, followed by strange grinding and crashing sounds below the deck. "Those are our watertight compartments closing," the captain explained. "It's an important part of our safety drill. In case of real trouble, water leaking into one compartment would not affect the rest of the ship. Even if we should collide with an iceberg, as did the *Titanic*, water rushing in will fill only that

"God leads us.
God will do the
right thing at the
right time. And
what a difference
that makes."

particular ruptured compartment. The ship, however, will still remain afloat."

When he spoke to the students at Yale, Osler remembered the captain's description of the boat:

Each one of you is certainly a much more marvelous organization than that great liner and bound on a far longer voyage. What I urge is that you learn to master your life by living each day in a day-tight compartment and this will certainly ensure your safety throughout your entire journey of life. Touch a button and hear, at every level of your life, the iron doors shutting out the Past—the dead yesterdays. Touch another and shut off, with a metal curtain, the Future—the unborn tomorrows. Then you are safe—safe for today.

Think not of the amount to be accomplished, the difficulties to be overcome, but set earnestly at the little task near your elbow, letting that be sufficient for the day; for surely our plain duty is not to see what lies dimly at a distance but to do what lies clearly at hand.[1]

Jesus made the same point in fewer words: "So don't worry about tomorrow, because tomorrow will have its own worries. Each day has enough trouble of its own" (Matt. 6:34).

Easy to say. Not always easy to do, right? We are so prone to worry. Just last night I was worrying in my sleep. I dreamed that I was diagnosed with ALS, a degenerative muscle disease, which took the life of my father. I awakened from the dream and, right there in the middle of the night,

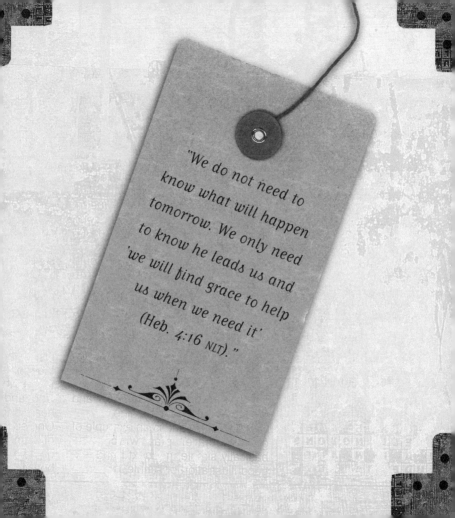

"We do not need to know what will happen tomorrow. We only need to know he leads us and 'we will find grace to help us when we need it' (Heb. 4:16 NLT)."

began to worry. Then Jesus' words came to my mind: "Don't worry about tomorrow." And for once, I decided not to. I dropped the burlap sack. After all, why let tomorrow's imaginary problem rob tonight's rest? Can I prevent the disease by staying awake? Will I postpone the affliction by thinking about it? Of course not. So I did the most spiritual thing I could have done. I went back to sleep.

Why don't you do the same? God is leading you. Leave tomorrow's problems until tomorrow.

Arthur Hays Sulzberger was the publisher of the *New York Times* during the Second World War. Because of the world conflict, he found it almost impossible to sleep. He was never able to banish worries from his mind until he adopted as his motto these five words—"one step enough for me"—taken from the hymn "Lead Kindly Light."[2]

Lead, kindly Light. . . .
Keep Thou my feet; I do not ask to see
The distant scene; one step enough for me.

God isn't going to let you see the distant scene either. So you might as well quit looking for it. He promises a lamp unto our feet, not a crystal ball into the future.[3] We do not need to know what will happen tomorrow. We only need to know he leads us and "we will find grace to help us when we need it" (Heb. 4:16 NLT).

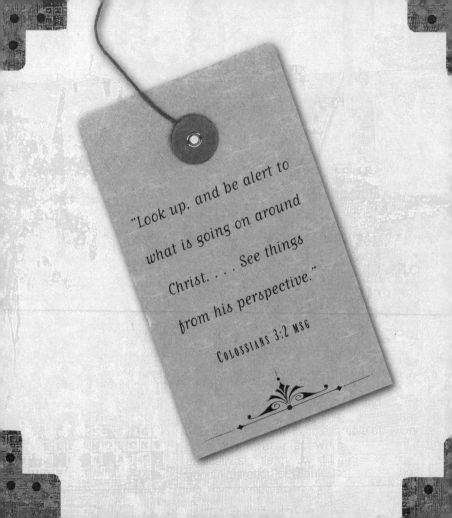

"Look up, and be alert to what is going on around Christ. . . . See things from his perspective."

COLOSSIANS 3:2 MSG

IT'S A JUNGLE OUT THERE

The Burden of Hopelessness

He restores my soul.

—PSALM 23:3 NKJV

I wonder if you could imagine yourself in a jungle. A dense jungle. A dark jungle. Your friends convinced you it was time for a once-in-a-lifetime trip, and here you are. You paid the fare. You crossed the ocean. You hired the guide and joined the group. And you ventured where you had never ventured before—into the thick, strange world of the jungle.

Sound interesting? Let's take it a step farther. Imagine that you are in the jungle, lost and alone. You paused to lace your boot, and when you looked up, no one was near. You took a chance and went to the right; now you're wondering if the others went to the left. (Or did you go left and they went right?)

Whatever, you are alone. And you have been alone for, well, you don't know how long it has been. Your watch was attached to your pack, and your pack is on the shoulder of the nice guy from New Jersey who volunteered to hold it while you tied your boots. You didn't intend for him to walk off with it. But he did. And here you are, in the jungle, with no clue how to get out.

You have a problem. First, you were not made for this place. Drop you in the center of avenues and buildings, and you could sniff your way home. But here in sky-blocking foliage? Here in trail-hiding thickets? You are out of your element. You weren't made for this jungle.

What's worse, you aren't equipped. You have no machete. No knife. No matches. No flares. No food. You aren't equipped, but now you are trapped—and you haven't a clue how to get out.

Sound like fun to you? Me neither. Before moving on, let's pause and ask how you would feel. Given such circumstances, what emotions would surface? With what thoughts would you wrestle?

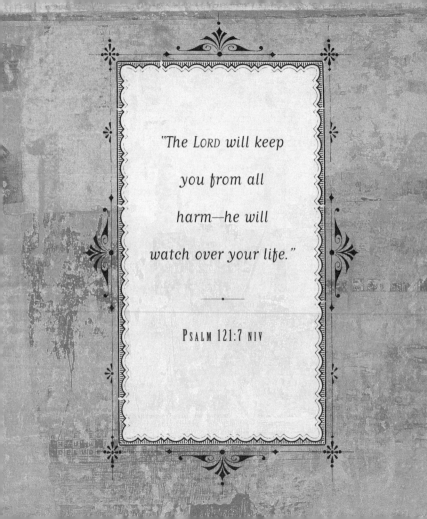

"The LORD will keep you from all harm—he will watch over your life."

PSALM 121:7 NIV

Fear? Of course you would.

Anxiety? To say the least.

Anger? I could understand that. (You'd like to get your hands on those folks who convinced you to take this trip.)

But most of all, what about hopelessness? No idea where to turn. No hunch what to do. Who could blame you for sitting on a log (better check for snakes first), burying your face in your hands, and thinking, *I'll never get out of here.* You have no direction, no equipment, no hope.

Can you freeze-frame that emotion for a moment? Can you sense, for just a second, how it feels to be out of your element? Out of solutions? Out of ideas and energy? Can you imagine, just for a moment, how it feels to be out of hope?

If you can, you can relate to many people in this world. For many people, life is—well, life is a jungle. Not a jungle of trees and beasts. Would that it were so simple. Would that our jungles could be cut with a machete or our adversaries trapped in a cage. But our jungles are comprised of the thicker thickets of failing health, broken hearts, and empty wallets. Our forests are framed with hospital walls and divorce courts. We don't hear the screeching of birds or the roaring of lions, but we do hear the complaints of neighbors and the demands of bosses. Our predators are our creditors, and the brush that surrounds us is the rush that exhausts us.

It's a jungle out there.

And for some, even for many, hope is in short supply. Hopelessness is an odd bag. Unlike the others, it isn't full. It is empty, and its emptiness creates the burden. Unzip the top and examine all the pockets. Turn it upside down and shake it hard. The bag of hopelessness is painfully empty.

"If you have
a person with
direction—who can
take you from this
place to the right
place—ah, then you
have one who can
restore your hope."

TICKET: | DATE:

TRAVELING LIGHT

Not a very pretty picture, is it? Let's see if we can brighten it up. We've imagined the emotions of being lost; you think we can do the same with being rescued? What would it take to restore your hope? What would you need to reenergize your journey?

Though the answers are abundant, three come quickly to mind.

The first would be a person. Not just any person. You don't need someone equally confused. You need someone who knows the way out.

And from him you need some vision. You need someone to lift your spirits. You need someone to look you in the face and say, "This isn't the end. Don't give up. There is a better place than this. And I'll lead you there."

And, perhaps most important, you need direction. If

you have only a person but no renewed vision, all you have is company. If he has a vision but no direction, you have a dreamer for company. But if you have a person with direction—who can take you from this place to the right place—ah, then you have one who can restore your hope.

Or, to use David's words, "He restores my soul."

Our Shepherd majors in restoring hope to the soul. Whether you are a lamb lost on a craggy ledge or a city slicker alone in a deep jungle, everything changes when your rescuer appears.

Your loneliness diminishes, because you have fellowship.

Your despair decreases, because you have vision.

Your confusion begins to lift, because you have direction.

Please note: You haven't left the jungle. The trees still

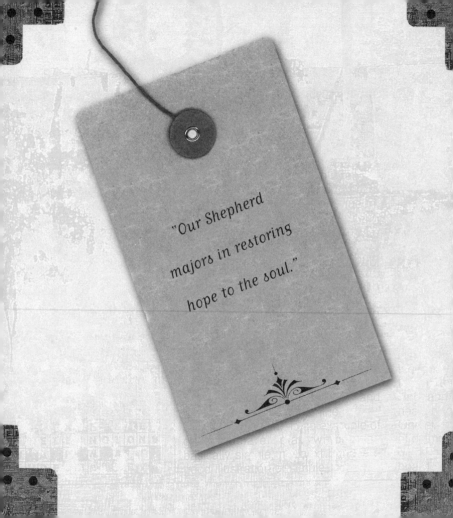

"Our Shepherd majors in restoring hope to the soul."

eclipse the sky, and the thorns still cut the skin. Animals lurk and rodents scurry. The jungle is still a jungle. It hasn't changed, but you have. You have changed because you have hope. And you have hope because you have met someone who can lead you out.

Your Shepherd knows that you were not made for this place. He knows you are not equipped for this place. So he has come to guide you out.

He has come to restore your soul. He is the perfect one to do so.

He has the right vision. He reminds you that "you are like foreigners and strangers in this world" (1 Pet. 2:11). And he urges you to lift your eyes from the jungle around you to the heaven above you. "Don't shuffle along, eyes to the ground, absorbed with the things right in front of you. Look up, and be alert to what is going on around Christ. . . . See things from his perspective" (Col. 3:2 MSG).

David said it this way: "I lift up my eyes to the hills—where does my help come from? My help comes from the LORD, the Maker of heaven and earth. He will not let your foot slip—he who watches over you will not slumber. . . . The LORD watches over you . . . the sun will not harm you by day, nor the moon by night. The LORD will keep you from all harm—he will watch over your life" (Ps. 121:1–7 NIV).

God, your rescuer, has the right vision. He also has the right direction. He made the boldest claim in the history of man when he declared, "I am the way" (John 14:6). People wondered if the claim was accurate. He answered their questions by cutting a path through the underbrush of sin and death . . . and escaped alive. He's the only one who ever

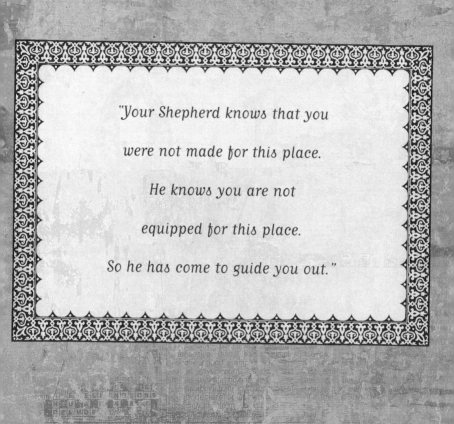

"Your Shepherd knows that you

were not made for this place.

He knows you are not

equipped for this place.

So he has come to guide you out."

did. And he is the only one who can help you and me do the same.

He has the right vision: He has seen the homeland. He has the right directions: He has cut the path. But most of all, he is the right person, for he is our God. Who knows the jungle better than the One who made it? And who knows the pitfalls of the path better than the One who has walked it?

The story is told of a man on an African safari deep in the jungle. The guide before him had a machete and was whacking away the tall weeds and thick underbrush. The traveler, wearied and hot, asked in frustration, "Where are we? Do you know where you are taking me? Where is the path?!" The seasoned guide stopped and looked back at the man and replied, "I am the path."

We ask the same questions, don't we? We ask God,

"Where are you taking me? Where is the path?" And he, like the guide, doesn't tell us. Oh, he may give us a hint or two, but that's all. If he did, would we understand? Would we comprehend our location? No, like the traveler, we are unacquainted with this jungle. So rather than give us an answer, Jesus gives us a far greater gift. He gives us himself.

Does he remove the jungle? No, the vegetation is still thick.

Does he purge the predators? No, danger still lurks.

Jesus doesn't give hope by changing the jungle; he restores our hope by giving us himself. And he has promised to stay until the very end. "I am with you always, to the very end of the age" (Matt. 28:20 NIV).

We need that reminder. We all need that reminder. For all of us need hope.

Some of you don't need it right now. Your jungle has become a meadow and your journey a delight. If such is the case, congratulations. But remember—we do not know what tomorrow holds. We do not know where this road will lead. You may be one turn from a cemetery, from a hospital bed, from an empty house. You may be a bend in the road from a jungle.

And though you don't need your hope restored today, you may tomorrow. And you need to know to whom you will turn.

Or perhaps you do need hope today. You know you were not made for this place. You know you are not equipped. You want someone to lead you out.

If so, call out for your Shepherd. He knows your voice. And he's just waiting for your request.

seven

A HEAVENLY EXCHANGE

The Burden of Guilt

He leads me in the paths of

righteousness for His name's sake.

—PSALM 23:3 NKJV

A friend organized a Christmas cookie swap for our church office staff. The plan was simple. Price of

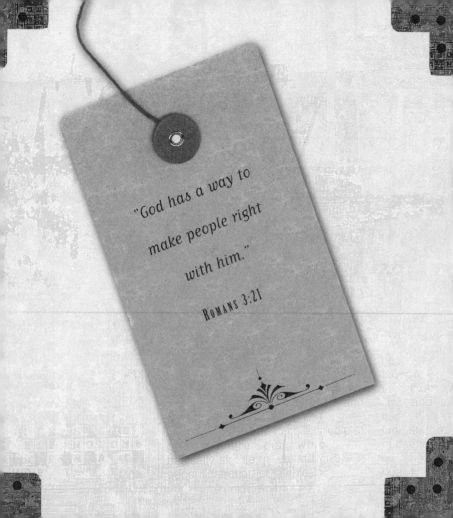

"God has a way to make people right with him."

ROMANS 3:21

admission was a tray of cookies. Your tray entitled you to pick cookies from the other trays. You could leave with as many cookies as you brought.

Sounds simple, if you know how to cook. But what if you can't? What if you can't tell a pan from a pot? What if, like me, you are culinarily challenged? What if you're as comfortable in an apron as a bodybuilder in a tutu? If such is the case, you've got a problem.

Such was the case, and I had a problem. I had no cookies to bring; hence I would have no place at the party. I would be left out, turned away, shunned, eschewed, and dismissed. (Are you feeling sorry for me yet?)

This was my plight.

And, forgive me for bringing it up, but your plight's even worse.

God is planning a party . . . a party to end all parties. Not a cookie party, but a feast. Not giggles and chitchat in the conference room, but wide-eyed wonder in the throne room of God.

Yes, the guest list is impressive. Your question to Jonah about undergoing a gut check in a fish gut? You'll be able to ask him. But more impressive than the names of the guests is the nature of the guests. No egos, no power plays. Guilt, shame, and sorrow will be checked at the gate. Disease, death, and depression will be the Black Plagues of a distant past. What we now see daily, there we will never see.

And what we now see vaguely, there we will see clearly. We will see God. Not by faith. Not through the eyes of Moses or Abraham or David. Not via Scripture or sunsets or summer rains. We will see not God's work or words, but

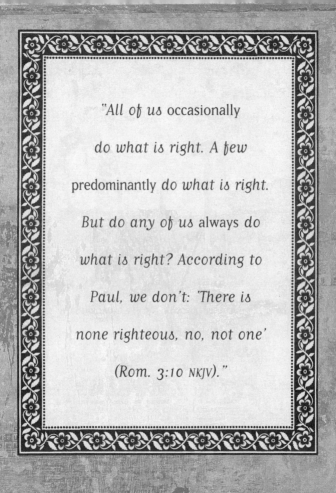

"All of us occasionally do what is right. A few predominantly do what is right. But do any of us always do what is right? According to Paul, we don't: 'There is none righteous, no, not one' (Rom. 3:10 NKJV)."

we will see him! For he is not the host of the party; he *is* the party. His goodness is the banquet. His voice is the music. His radiance is the light, and his love is the endless topic of discussion.

There is only one hitch. The price of admission is somewhat steep. In order to come to the party, you need to be righteous. Not good. Not decent. Not a taxpayer or churchgoer.

Citizens of heaven are righteous. R-i-g-h-t.

All of us *occasionally* do what is right. A few *predominantly* do what is right. But do any of us *always* do what is right? According to Paul, we don't: "There is none righteous, no, not one" (Rom. 3:10 NKJV).

Paul is adamant about this. He goes on to say, "No one anywhere has kept on doing what is right; not one" (Rom. 3:12 TLB).

Some may beg to differ. "I'm not perfect, Max, but I'm better than most folks. I've led a good life. I don't break the rules. I don't break hearts. I help people. I like people. Compared to others, I think I could say I'm a righteous person."

I used to try that one on my mother. She'd tell me my room wasn't clean, and I'd ask her to go with me to my brother's room. His was always messier than mine. "See, my room is clean; just look at his."

Never worked. She'd walk me down the hall to her room. When it came to tidy rooms, my mom was righteous. Her closet was just right. Her bed was just right. Her bathroom was just right. Compared to hers, my room was, well, just wrong. She would show me her room and say, "This is what I mean by clean."

"For Christ died for
sins once for all, the
righteous for the
unrighteous, to
bring you to God."

1 PETER 3:18 NIV

TICKET: DATE:

TRAVELING   LIGHT

God does the same. He points to himself and says, "This is what I mean by righteousness."

Righteousness is who God is.

"Our God and Savior Jesus Christ does what is right" (2 Pet. 1:1).

"God is a righteous judge" (Ps. 7:11 NIV).

"The LORD is righteous, he loves justice" (Ps. 11:7 NIV).

God's righteousness "endures forever" (Ps. 112:3 NIV) and "reaches to the skies" (Ps. 71:19 NIV).

Isaiah described God as "a righteous God and a Savior" (Isa. 45:21 NIV).

On the eve of his death, Jesus began his prayer with the words "Righteous Father" (John 17:25 NIV).

Get the point? God is righteous. His decrees are righteous (Rom. 1:32). His judgment is righteous (Rom. 2:5).

His requirements are righteous (Rom. 8:4). His acts are righteous (Dan. 9:16). Daniel declared, "Our God is right in everything he does" (Dan. 9:14).

God is never wrong. He has never rendered a wrong decision, experienced the wrong attitude, taken the wrong path, said the wrong thing, or acted the wrong way. He is never too late or too early, too loud or too soft, too fast or too slow. He has always been and always will be right. He is righteous.

When it comes to righteousness, God runs the table without so much as a bank shot. And when it comes to righteousness, we don't know which end of the cue stick to hold. Hence, our plight.

Will God, who is righteous, spend eternity with those who are not? Would Harvard admit a third-grade dropout?

"Calvary is the compost pile for guilt."

If it did, the act might be benevolent, but it wouldn't be right. If God accepted the unrighteous, the invitation would be even nicer, but would he be right? Would he be right to overlook our sins? Lower his standards? No. He wouldn't be right. And if God is anything, he is right.

He told Isaiah that righteousness would be his plumb line, the standard by which his house is measured (Isa. 28:17). If we are unrighteous, then, we are left in the hallway with no cookies. Or to use Paul's analogy, "we're sinners, every one of us, in the same sinking boat with everybody else" (Rom. 3:19 MSG). Then what are we to do?

Carry a load of guilt? Many do. So many do.

What if our spiritual baggage were visible? Suppose the luggage in our hearts was literal luggage on the street. You know what you'd see most of all? Suitcases of guilt.

Bags bulging with binges, blowups, and compromises. Look around you. The fellow in the gray-flannel suit? He's dragging a decade of regrets. The kid with the baggy jeans and nose ring? He'd give anything to retract the words he said to his mother. But he can't. So he tows them along. The woman in the business suit? Looks as if she could run for senator? She'd rather run for help, but she can't run at all. Not hauling that carpetbag of cagmag everywhere she goes.

Listen. The weight of weariness pulls you down. Self-reliance misleads you. Disappointments discourage you. Anxiety plagues you. But guilt? Guilt consumes you.

So what do we do? Our Lord is right, and we are wrong. His party is for the guiltless, and we are anything but. What do we do?

I can tell you what I did. I confessed my need. Remember my cookie dilemma? This is the e-mail I sent to the whole staff: "I can't cook, so I can't be at the party."

Did any of the assistants have mercy on me? No.

Did any of the staff have mercy on me? No.

Did any of the Supreme Court justices have mercy on me? No.

But a saintly sister in the church did have mercy on me. How she heard of my problem, I do not know. Perhaps my name found its way onto an emergency prayer list. But I do know this. Only moments before the celebration, I was given a gift, a plate of cookies, twelve circles of kindness.

And by virtue of that gift, I was privileged a place at the party.

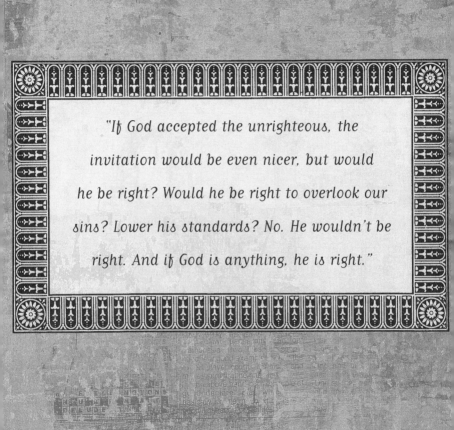

"If God accepted the unrighteous, the invitation would be even nicer, but would he be right? Would he be right to overlook our sins? Lower his standards? No. He wouldn't be right. And if God is anything, he is right."

Did I go? You bet your cookies I did. Like a prince carrying a crown on a pillow, I carried my gift into the room, set it on the table, and stood tall. And because some good soul heard my plea, I was given a place at the table.

And because God hears your plea, you'll be given the same. Only, he did more—oh, so much more—than bake cookies for you.

It was, at once, history's most beautiful and most horrible moment. Jesus stood in the tribunal of heaven. Sweeping a hand over all creation, he pleaded, "Punish me for their mistakes. See the murderer? Give me his penalty. The adulteress? I'll take her shame. The bigot, the liar, the thief? Do to me what you would do to them. Treat me as you would a sinner."

And God did. "For Christ died for sins once for all, the

righteous for the unrighteous, to bring you to God" (1 Pet. 3:18 NIV).

Yes, righteousness is what God is, and, yes, righteousness is what we are not, and, yes, righteousness is what God requires. But "God has a way to make people right with him" (Rom. 3:21).

David said it like this: "He leads me in the paths of righteousness" (Ps. 23:3 NKJV).

The path of righteousness is a narrow, winding trail up a steep hill. At the top of the hill is a cross. At the base of the cross are bags. Countless bags full of innumerable sins. Calvary is the compost pile for guilt. Would you like to leave yours there as well?

One final thought about the Christmas cookie party. Did everyone know I didn't bake the cookies? If they didn't, I told them. I told them I was present by virtue of someone else's work. My only contribution was my own confession.

We'll be saying the same for eternity.

Notes

Chapter 3: The Prison of Want

1. Randy C. Alcorn, *Money, Possessions, and Eternity* (Wheaton, Ill.: Tyndale Publishers, 1989), 55.

2. Chris Seidman, *Little Buddy* (Orange, Calif.: New Leaf Books, 2001), 138. Used with permission.

3. Rick Atchley, "I Have Learned the Secret," audio-tape 7 of the 1997 Pepperdine Lectures (Malibu, Calif., 1997). Used with permission.

Chapter 4: I Will Give You Rest

1. Robert Sullivan, "Sleepless in America," *Life*, February 1998, 56–66; and *Prime Time Live*, 2 March 1998.

2. Sullivan, "Sleepless," 63.

3. Ibid.

4. Phillip Keller, *A Shepherd Looks at Psalm 23* (Grand Rapids: Mich.: Zondervan Publishing, 1970; reprint in *Phillip Keller: The Inspirational Writings*, New York: Inspirational Press, 1993), 28–29 (page citations are from the reprint edition).

5. Helmut Thielicke, *Encounter with Spurgeon*, trans. John W. Doberstein (Philadelphia: Fortress Press, 1963; reprint, Grand Rapids, Mich.: Baker Book House, 1975), 220 (page citation is from the reprint edition).

Chapter 5: Whaddifs and Howells

1. Og Mandino, *The Spellbinder's Gift* (New York: Fawcett Columbine, 1995), 70–71.

2. From "Worrier and Warrior," a sermon by Ted Schroder, Christ Episcopal Church, San Antonio, Texas, on 10 April 1994.

3. See Psalm 119:105.